NTOMBENTLE:
SELECTED POEMS

Sithembele Isaac Xhegwana

Mwanaka Media and Publishing Pvt Ltd,
Chitungwiza Zimbabwe
*
Creativity, Wisdom and Beauty

Publisher: *Mmap*
Mwanaka Media and Publishing Pvt Ltd
24 Svosve Road, Zengeza 1
Chitungwiza Zimbabwe
mwanaka@yahoo.com
mwanaka13@gmail.com
www.africanbookscollective.com/publishers/mwanaka-media-and-publishing
https://facebook.com/MwanakaMediaAndPublishing/

Distributed in and outside N. America by African Books Collective
orders@africanbookscollective.com
www.africanbookscollective.com

ISBN: 978-1-77928-210-1
EAN: 9781779282101

© Sithembele Isaac Xhegwana 2025

All rights reserved.
No part of this book may be reproduced or transmitted in any form or by any means, mechanical or electronic, including photocopying and recording, or be stored in any information storage or retrieval system, without written permission from the publisher

DISCLAIMER
All views expressed in this publication are those of the author and do not necessarily reflect the views of *Mmap*.

Contents

Introduction 6
NTOMBENTLE 11
BELATED LOVE 15
THE BELL RINGER 17
ON THESE MOUNTAINS 19
COME BACK HOME 21
ANGELA 23
LOST POEM 25
LAST POEM 27
CONFESSIONS OF A WANDERER 28
CLASSICAL MOMENTS 30
KHOLEKA 31
NOPASI 33
NOPASI'S LAMENT 37
NGXINGXOLO 40
THE LAST SONG 43
HINTSA'S PORTRAIT 45
KING SHAKA OF THE ZULUS 46
QUESTIONS OF IDENTITY 49
RITES OF PASSAGE 51
OSTRICH EGG CARRIER OF THE KALAHARI 53

STRUGGLES OF MEMORY	55
DEATH WISH	57
TO HIMSELF	59
HOMECOMING	62
THE RETURN	64
DAYBREAK	68
PRAYER	69
REFUSING TO WORSHIP	70
MAINSTAY	72
THE VILLAGE CARNIVAL	76
MEDITATING	77
AT THE END OF THE JOURNEY	81
TO STEPHEN WATSON	83
SCATTERED FEATHERS	84
LAND OF THORNS	85
THE CAPTURED MAIDEN	87
IN THE MEMORY OF MAKHANDA	90
MY FATHER'S SPEAR	93
A LETTER TO THUTHULA	96
WHEN I USED TO DREAM	98
THE MAIDEN RETURNS	99
VOICES FROM WITHIN	100

PRAYER TO ULU (AFTER CHINUA ACHEBE'S ARROW OF GOD) 101
AT THE GATES OF XHOSALAND 103
THE LEO MARQUARD NECKTIE 105
NOMTSHWEBELELE'S STONE 107
AT EVENING 109
MAMLAMBO 110
Mmap New African Poets Series 112

Introduction

"The past is a foreign country; they do things differently there". The opening words of L.P. Hartley's 1953 novel, *The Go-Between*, resonate paradoxically with this new selection of Xhegwana's poetry. The past can always be captured and pondered as stolid academic history, objectively open to debate and continuous refinement. It can also become a romantic emotional backdrop to everyday existence.

But what if history still lives in us as an imagined daily reality? Not foreign, not objective, not constructed, but dancingly alive in our everyday life? This seems to me the premise of this powerful collection.

Stories and episodes remembered, or half remembered, by future readers from the published histories of, say, Theal, Macmillan, Peires, or Etherington, or creative evocations associated with poets such as Dhlomo, Mqhayi or Mann – to cite fairly arbitrary examples – come to life here as the mental furniture of a unique individual. These stories and episodes inhabit a sensibility struggling to relate past and present without neglecting either. The poet welcomes the reader into his inner world, caught in a relentless dialogue between today and yesterday.

It matters not whether the reader is steeped in South African history, especially that of Xhosaland in the nineteenth century or today's Eastern Cape. The poetry speaks "as if" we are part of the experiences evoked and, in the end, we are. The poet's past becomes, for the reader, an inhabited zone, no longer L.P. Hartley's foreign country.

At the gates of Xhosaland we have come,

empty handed we stand.
From far away we come,
with imaginary landscapes
as the only precursors of our path.
("At The Gates of Xhosaland")

We meet important historical figures and their stories, but only as they feature in the poet's consciousness. For instance, he finds himself honouring the great warrior Makhanda, while struggling to let go of this hero's seemingly doomed mission, or condemning the "liberal charlatans" of King William's Town (now Qonce) who stood by unknowingly as Steve Biko was tortured and murdered. Did they even *want* to know? The poet does not shrink from picking at painful historical scars such as King Hintsa's severed head being exported to Britain. (I mean, *who does that?*) We make a detour to the northern Nguni in a scathing celebration of King Shaka, beautifully crafted, but more a horrified indictment than laudatory praise.

Bruising wars are reprised for their enduring effects: the War of the Axe, the War of Mlanjeni, the War of Nxele, the War of Thuthula ("The Return"). Nongqawuse and Thuthula are correctly exculpated. They were maneuvered (by whom, the poet remains silent). History points to the "prophet", Mhlakaza, being at the heart of the Cattle-Killing, with poor Thuthula caught between feuding royal rivals and taking blame for the conflict named after her, rather like Helen of Sparta in the Trojan Wars. The poet makes amends to the two women in fitting poetic tributes.

But these poems are no stodgy historical recapitulation. Some of them are bewilderingly beautiful, wonderful realisations of an art form. Xhegwana writes self-deprecatingly:

My chants were only sung
To raise myself above disorders
That only issues of predisposition
Could lay claim on.
("At the End of the Journey")

    Au contraire, these are considered poems of wandering and wondering, seeking some resolution of the two congruent modes. The poet's life floats in living history, his own and that of his people, poignant stories and their life-worlds thrumming relentlessly in his present day consciousness. To help fill an inner void, the poet searches for his own family's past, his cultural and ancestral roots, a missing father and his abandoned mother. But these are merely concrete instantiations of a deeper spiritual dislocation. Ultimately the poetic search goes back to humanity's genesis:

    Once upon a time, our fires burned
tall, their flames opening the darkness –
as we chanted. Dancing, we unveiled
the reservoirs of our light.

There, our feet tattooing, we chased
the moon. We chased the blue buck,
the eland. We raced with the Bushmen
and the Khoi – even as far as the red
pillars of the stormy skylines.

We watched our high priests, sangomas,
negotiating with clouds.
("Genesis")
Throughout this technically accomplished collection sounds the call of home, the longing for a particular loved person, for known

landscapes, the realm of the ancestors, an elastic pull that draws and centers the speaker. Alienated physically and spiritually, the poet has suffered from manic depression, becoming sadly conversant with a regime of psychiatric drugs ("Lithium, Lagatil, and others") and horrible mental isolation. Stronger than the centripetal force of these bipolar episodes is the immemorial pull of home. There are lost loves, abandoned relationships, a litany of estrangement to be overcome. And still there is the search for faith:

> Eternal Spirit, lift us higher than the trees,
> Make us see the fires beneath the earth.
> Make us walk more slowly than our fleeting breath.
> Plant us in your passages
> Beyond sacrificial blood and wooden temples.
> ("Prayer")

Sometimes we meet poems of simple observation, reminiscent of Wordsworth, such as "Ostrich Egg Carrier of the Kalahari", while "Rites of Passage", which describes an initiate's underwater visit to *aBantu bomlambo*, the people of the river, adventitiously but somehow appropriately, presents a visual image reminiscent of Millais' famous painting of the death of Ophelia. Reading poetry is not a tidy business.

Perhaps poems of revisitation are the heart of the collection, where the poet returns to the site of his former suffering:

I have been to places
Where no mother's love
Could fetch me.

I have wandered,
Like a vagabond,
In and out of institutions.

("To Himself")

The poet's story is all there. I won't recount it, because you need to hear it in the poet's own word-rhythms: the songs of returning home to the place "where all guilt begins".
This wonderful collection includes a moving tribute to the poet's creative writing mentor at the University of Cape Town, the late Stephen Watson. His teacher would be proud.

Laurence Wright
Simon's Town
March 2025

NTOMBENTLE[1]

Deified from generation to generation
My deserted citadel and ancient palace
Covered by the blue skies
Carved deep in sharp rocks,
    caves
Floundering in sapphire forest-mountains
Thick reeds
Whose abode are sun-married rivers.

I am a country beauty
Forsaken by a once prominent
    village royalty
Reclined here still
Surviving from the blows
In deep mourning for *Baba*
My most arrogant lover.

Endless panorama of distinct groves
Caravans of camels scattered all over
Dragged by desert luminaries,
Decorated in ivory and gold
Scores of women infiltrating my palace
First born wife kicked out
My only sin a flat refusal
For my love
To compete with many others
For the attention of his highness.

---

[1] Based on a Xhosa folksong by the same name.

Still here I am
After centuries of seclusion
    and solitude
Absorbed by a wind shaken grave
With only my two thin feet visible
Still
With much beauty shimmering
Sun-married, absorbing this kingdom.

Almost a custom
Now,
A pilgrimage to a faraway goddess
Young men bestowing posthumous honour
Showering me with all kinds of praises.
With the hope
Of winning my love.

My refusal
To remove myself from these deep natural abodes
Still remaining as a secret
As royal men documented history
Refused to capture such
Only surrogates seem to claim my story
Oratures from these love-struck
    young men
Throw all kinds of tribute on my way
Again
Hoping to win my love.

I am not of their age
Nor of their territory
Brough here by mercifully water tides
From shores far away.

Will these sharp winds continue digging
my grave?
By day and by night?

Maybe I should recover from this
dangerous ciesta
Of retracing the footsteps
Of the millions of young men
Who after every twelve full
    moons
Ascend the mountain
To honour my invisible grave site.

I do not have love for them
I only comprehend such from
    the far-away past
And the great kingdom
Below my inconsequential grave
I will refuse, I refuse
To be demonised by this
Institutionalised misconception
    of love.

              ****

Now defunct
My origins are of the many nations
    and tribes
Hidden beyond those crumbled
    ivory thrones
Catapulted from times not captured
    by the Gregorian calendar
Spat out through legendary mouths
    of fables and myths.

Transfigured
Camouflaged within nature's ironic
    splendour
Young beauty, transfigured from times
    past
I refuse to be marked down
I have been told
To overcome the trance suffocating me
    in these many abodes.

I have never been destitute
In my own accord
As I have already alluded
In my previous life
I refused to be made first
Or second in line.
Therefore
My love is not worth of any man
    here
 Please leave me alone
Let my spirit rest
And my solitude be embraced
In this temple of my invisible body.

BELATED LOVE

Returning home, endeavouring
to apprehend preceding acquaintances
proves close to be unattainable. Moving
on at your side, procrastinates all

the possible reunions, especially
that you have moved on, a rebel,
on your own. Journeys of self-
discovery get crowned into

different kinds of love. It is
close to comprehensible that you
are no longer at the same spot
where I left you, folded up like

an almost creased grass mat
behind that wind-whipped
village door. Yes, rekindling
conflagrations from the past

seems to be very much
impossible. Between us,
a physical impediment
has been enacted. While

rekindling the past analogous
connections seems impossible,
one way or another, we can still
reach out to each other. Even if

it's not the same as before,

we can still maintain a
connection and still dictated
by the 'walled in' distance

we can still support each
other, and maybe under
veiled circumstances,
love each other. Now

that I know, that the pend-
ulum of life-cycles constantly
swings towards growth
and change and that connect-

ions evolve into new forms
of indulgence, I am not giving
up on us and this journey
of discovery and self-

enlightenment, not just
physically, but also
spiritually and vocational.

THE BELL RINGER

In the memory of Dr Lech Kowalski

The last time he rang the bell
at the cathedral, was just after
I saw him in his consulting
room. When I came back

to consult I was greeted
by the news that he was gone,
never to come back. Yes, he
was old but he still loved

scuba-diving and other
rituals that were so sacred
to him, like ringing the bell
of that sky-tall building

in the middle of the city.
Tall as the sky, he used
to reach out his arms
and offer me his elbow

as a form of greeting -
new rules dictated
by a masked disease.
I can still hear the

constellation of
bells that were rung
in his honour. I still

shake frantically when

I see his framed picture
hanging from the clustered
wall of his office.

ON THESE MOUNTAINS

You distant mountains, a conglomeration
of mystic forests and deep caves, Hoho forests,
purchased by a destitute Xhosa king. Multitudes,
innumerable herds of cattle, a pact with a Khoi-
san queen, Hoho. A fort for warring warriors,
hidden in those ghostly caves and forests,
running away from aggressive English armies,
even serpentine amaXhosa warriors. Ngqika
and Ndlambe warring in the Amalinda's, the
biggest amaXhosa civil war ever, Xhosa
warrior killing another Xhosa warrior. Not
over the land, a love triangle over Thuthula,
Mthunzana's highly prized daughter. You
could never be a sanctuary, we only had
to run away as clouds of terror settled,
we would not pretend you were a
comforter, nor could we seek inspiration
from you.

You distant mountains, even if we did
encapsulate from the fragments of our
imagination, endless paths invading
your aggressive groves. To us you meant
horrors, endless nightmares were invoked,
in the presence of the mystic Gwadana,
a rumoured abode for Xhosa black magic.
In the towering shades of Ntaba kaNdoda,
with its hidden tombs and scattered bones
of our desolate kings and chiefs,
who not only died painful and lonesome

deaths, but whose narratives were appropriated by shameless and never ending dictatorships.

Shameful mountains, what meaning could you have to us, other than that imposed by colonial and separate development harbingers?

COME BACK HOME

My son, for many moons now have
you turned your back on our moonlight,
piggy-backing on the bellowing waves
of those many waters. Hardly do you

write, often my breath refuses to have
the same pulse as that of the wandering
wind. As you stand there beneath those
distant shadows spilled out by those

mountains, here I toil in the land of
the litany of my forebears that your
uncle decorated in all colours. Those
peasant hands, now creased beneath

this blistering sunshine, many layers
below this shaking earth, attest to a
belated love I once held for my people
and my land. Hardly have I seen the

winter sun slowly hiding beyond
those western horizons, making
way for the spring thunder bolts
and summer rains that always

break the sun-scorched surface
of our landscape. My son, come
back home. Perhaps, a new song
will emanate from the mountain

crests, the crown of our mountains,
overlooking our mist-hovered
rondavels. Come back home,
to light the fires that are already
flickering –

maybe the congested ice
embracing these hills may
let go of us. Come back
home, please come back.

ANGELA

How was I supposed to know that Angela was a twin, and that
for a life-time she had not cast her shadow by the riverside?
They told me. Only after the post-mortem. That the physician

declared the diagnosis and the motive. Angela is a twin. And
her partner had danced all the way to heaven or hell. She never
saw him or played with him along the sacred Westminster

gothic temples. The savage lured him before the break of dawn;
he vanished before the midwife could cut the cord. Angela
grew up; she was told how tall her brother could have been

(had he been alive). From London she flew to Cape Town.
I met her while I was gathering reeds in the open fields.
She told me she had seen some along the River Thames;

they were fleshy (she said). I remembered that we
have many rivers in the archaic 'Xhosaland': the Kei,
the Orange, the Keiskamma, the Buffalo and the Debe.

We agreed to take a Greyhound bus to ' Xhosaland'
and gather reeds along the riverside. I only dreamt
of two things. That along the riverside I could collect

the reeds and that Angela could assist me. I never
planned to slaughter her. But here she is; dead. I
never slaughtered Angela, I swear. The old doctor

is convinced I have. He told me that I should not
have brought her by the river side. Angela

is a twin. Moreover, her partner danced away

to unknown territories. She is gone now. Is it fair
for Angela, that in the obituary the *Gothic Font*
declares: "She died collecting reeds with a male

stranger along the banks of an unknown river
in the far-away Xhosaland which lies at the bottom
part of that dark and wet Africa"? Why should I

be a mental prisoner , when I know I never drowned
or strangled her? I wonder, is my ignorance my very
indictment? Here is a million-dollar question and the

bone of contention. Did Angela die only because
she is a twin whose partner had flown away before
the break of dawn? Did she die because she was

an ignorant twin who paid a visit to her grave –
site only to be absorbed pre-maturely? Did
she die because she is Queen Victoria's

descendent who visited a river side
 in 'Xhosaland' only to harvest reeds
for commercial consumption

in Cape Town or London? Did I
drown or strangle her? In which
degree is my professed murder?

Please Angela, wake up. That
is all I can say before I claim
my position in that dark and wet cell.

LOST POEM

Would I, a son of a grieving 'Fingo' mother, burn out in desolation?
The sun rises, only to touch me with its fiery fingers. Will I be pushed out to a mere oblivion? Will I be crushed like an undiscovered diamond, with its glimmer shivering underneath a dust of those hungry for its glory. Will I be crushed, beneath the clumsy
feet of these merchants, as a black diamond, whose glory is enclosed
within dungeons of selfishness?

Mama, would you stand up from the dust under which you sleep, and march – and be my only spokesperson? For I cannot speak, only the whispers of death strangle me. Have you not heard my groans, in shuddering tones they all speak at once, to dig a shallow grave wherein they could hide my spoils.

The dark surfaces of the earth tremble, surely they shake, to lend me an ear to the sound of my desolate cries. I reach out, only to touch the wetness of the towering skies, they embrace me. I can lay down my life and utter those scarce words of promise, this wetness, this darkness, it is the only embryo in which my existence can rest and grow.

I crave for the light, I strive to touch the gentle warmth of the embracing skies. Will I be caressed in your dangling breasts, the only warmth I know, sweet dear mama?
Is it you spilling out lullabies from your crumbling lips?
I will disappear graceful with you holding my blistered hand. Hold me dear mama, in the face of the judgements

read out from the crystal-clear life tablets. This is all
they know. You can teach them better lessons,
such kind of truth has never evaded my consciousness.
A last line now mama, from this posthumous song
I have composed for you. Everyday, I hold dearly
on a cliff, I live in this big limbo where I hardly
learn about news from tomorrow. Would you stand
up from the dust under which you sleep, and be
my only advocate?

LAST POEM

The sleeping village
that never wakes up.
Only at the retracing
of many footsteps,
voices, hushed
from this tower
of silence cannot
be picked up.
Footsteps, still
in an eternity
had not been
heard. Bodies,
silent in memory
forgotten.

Contrary to my wishes
I have been enthroned
under these ancient skins
to be the vulture
of these timeless rites.
In my long forgotten
ancestral land
between earth and sky
covered in maggots
I hold, to many altars.

CONFESSIONS OF A WANDERER

I
There is a woman who waits
for me, somewhere she calls home.
She likes me to read her poems from Frost
each night; She likes to call me hers,
her own. But other things, it seems,
are always claiming me. The earth's
dust is seeking day after day
to swallow me.

I cannot stay here, in one place. The sea demon,
they say, is angry with me.
I am always on the go;
I always break the flow of the demon's plots
for my life.

II
I have searched, sometimes
it seems the whole world around,
for a thing not owned
My hands slipping, like Sisyphus
with that stone, again and again
as he attains, almost
the mountain-crest where he
at last can rest.

I have searched
under the very toes of the sea
I have jumped from that hanging cliff,
the mind, I have trampled in the
the lion's den, my fear. I

have embraced the burning bush
In vision upon vision, befriending
a thousand hills along the way,
talking to them, hearing the speech
of hills.

III
Even now
I can feel the earth,
How it shakes beneath my feet!
Those village witches are after me
Again; I must soon be gone! A stranger,
Almost in rags, wandering on
the mountains, citizen of another world
A race without a name or nationality,
Whose love is always
for some other thing.

CLASSICAL MOMENTS

Instead of sitting on this rock
as wave crashes upon wave,
I measure my own illusion:
a mood which drives me out

of the interiors, away from you.
Still, the smell of pine – not
the pine I see standing,
dark and scarry, well above
the river's bank – calls me

home. Back to the more
familiar setting: a two roomed
flat, a wall clock with its
pendulum busy breaking
stillness, you, folded on the
grass mat. It is to these

moments that my thoughts
shall sink deeper. Upon being
driven out in rain, the smell
of pine – the more refined,
domesticated – ushers
another instance – you -

A forebearer of a hope
that overcomes my moments
of polar madness.

KHOLEKA

My black silk doek has turned grey,
My German print dress has faded away.
I have abandoned the spot by the riverside;
These days, I draw water from poisonous taps.

Snakes have long invaded the village.
The red dust that itched our bodies
    hurries along with the river,
The commercial train passed early this morning,
    at six,
What about that fateful morning,
When you and the passenger train
left me behind?

In the village, the young boys knock at my door
    to invade your once sacred territory
I no longer can team up with married women
    to fetch wood
I have stopped writing, my fingers are dry,
My fires have burned me, our children
    have deserted me.

I wonder if my songs can still enchant you.
I wonder if I could still capture you
    with my wild dance.
Tata ka Sipho, I will meet you halfway
    in the obsolete passenger train station,
Please phone,
I will give you my new neighbour's
    phone number.

Please, don't forget to speak to Kholeka,
As I am now called by my maiden name,
Since I ran away
    from your most loving family.
For still brutalizing
My own freedom.

NOPASI

Long, long ago, somewhere in Xhosaland there was a young woman named Nopasi. The Xhosa gods had given her the gift of sanuse – chief sangoma – that would help restore the glory of the past. As usually with gifts of such a nature, she had to undergo "ukuthwasa". Hers was to be different, she had to be caught away by the spirits and be presented with the "white stone" which would be the essence of her glory. Someone also needed this stone, and Nopasi, for her own purposes…

The speaker in the poem is Nopasi's husband.

I

She used to fetch wood from Hoho
And turn it to a gold bundle and bring it home
And her fires never flickered.

II

These very stems have now pinched her
And she herself is in a bundle folded up
We are taking her back to the woods where she belonged.

III

She used to pack water from Keiskamma River
And drive it to her enamel container to bring it home
And children never thirsted.

IV

The very waters now have drowned her
And she can only be transported by wagons
We are taking her back to the water where her temple is.

V

The spirits that reside in wood and waters
The spirits that brood over Hoho and Keiskamma
The preservers of life, the guardians of death.

VI

Like a flame she walked like lightening she has vanished
Her tiny neck packed the wood and the fires
Her tender feet have already turned into stone.

VII

Like a crippled bull my cries are going to echo throughout Hoho,
    Ntabethemba and Ntabozuko
Even the Queen of the Oceans will shake in her mystical throne
I will invade Gwadana I will accompany the western shadows
    to their dens.

VIII

I will sing a song without any lyrics
I will feed the gods to anger them
I will embrace my cat skins, I will collect my knobkerries and
assegais

IX

I will ride my stallion Bhungani to Qholorha
I will stop every maid by the riverside
I will follow the shadows to their western nests.

X

Gonondo has to accompany me to Tsholomnqa
That is where Nopas's carcass innocently lies
Let her speak to the wind: let the fires sing her songs.

XI

I hear that Mlanjeni has captured her
He is dancing with her, he is stealing her to the clouds
Will she land in Nongqawuse's kraal and present her
    with my handkerchief?

XII

Myekeni u Nopasi ahambe
Kuba singqungqe sagqiba
Sazitsiba neziblalo zokumkani

XIII

Nopasi clinched in a wooden box: that is her second coming
I will not stop it, I will not vanish it: let it go
Throngs over there are waiting to welcome the maid.

XIV

Shaking gods of Gwadana what offerings could appease you?
I have the cattle the women and the children
I have the land the mealies and the pumpkins.
XV

Yonder the grey-headed chiefs are rounded up in a circle
The fire is burning the bull is bellowing
Nopasi has finally arrived: the mighty princess.

XVI

Darling! (We will meet in the dusk)
My darling! (We will meet in the dusk)
My darling! (We will meet in the dusk).

NOPASI'S LAMENT

Once I was a child, a girl
playing *puca* along the river's quiet.
Once a bird spoke, a hare passed by,
and, from the waters,
I saw people.

People came, encircling, trapping me.
My mother, father, called me sick.
But they had their demons,
They could not cast out my own.
Till I dreamt another dream.

I saw this woman,
They called her the Queen of the Oceans.
She held the key to the five great kingdoms.
She held the key to my dreams:
A sacred white stone.

Thus I followed
the shadow of the wind.
a crushed reed, I fell prey
to the cruel adventures
of the sea demon.
Yet I survived.

Once she heard
about my impending
sanuse graduation
the queen of the Oceans
gnashed her teeth.

I went through many fires,
For cleaning, so they say.
I plunged naked
into deep waters.
I ate and drank sour herbs.
I inhaled iron-red coals.
But I have a demon
they cannot cast out.
It tortures me, devours me.

My place is among
the lowest of the low
My kind will crouch along
like those low hills,
those mud huts
beyond the river.

The enemy is swift, her arrows sharp.
Warriors are pointing their sword,
The winds are tossing me
under the rocks
Where is the lion?
To take me across this dark river?

My spirit heavy, my mind
half-beaten, one breast
cut off, womanhood
defiled, where is the road
where the cold of grass, the stone,
will not bite my feet?
Where is the road
on which I might return?

My songs shall go to the silent, the alone.
My songs shall be this pledge to myself.
My songs shall break from tyranny,
The arrogance of chiefs,
of kings.

It is my song, my lament
that is my lion,
That will be my ferry —
A road to carry me across
the river's dark;
To sing me, and you too,
Back to the place of quiet water.

NGXINGXOLO

Ancestral sanctuary, whose mystic pool, like
a python-magnet, immersed prince Gcaleka
into the abode of the great water-*sanuse*.
At the bloom of 1778, in honour of the

young king, the mega-village over-
looking the twin landscape of the Kei,
abuzz with celebrations as the awaited
prince Gcaleka's return from the presence
of Somagwaza, the inventor of the man-

making ritual. The invisible retinue
of past Xhosa kings and men retainers
spiritually oblique, he was pulled
towards the stoned carpet of this
liminal zone, a twin mirror of the

historical and geographical conju-
ncture of Ngxingxolo, only that
in the stead of people are serpentines,
river people and river bound fauna
and flora. To appease the water bound

"kidnappers" of the soon to be king,
the fresh blood of a roaring bull
gushed out like a spring down
the lime dongas of this gigantic
river. Huge barrels filled to the

brim with sorghum foams,
sacred herbs indulged, only

fit for a future king's home-
coming celebration. A royal house
sanuse officiating the assembly,

floating above the lifted hands of the
shimmering waters, enroute the
concealed abode of the faded
prince, a lion kareose, *umnweba*,
venerated kingship stuff and relics

of a regal Xhosa throne. Like a sky
snake, *inkanyamba*, winding
around a coastal village bearing
the same name, Ngxingxolo, epi-
centre of Xhosa long-told epic

narratives. Kinship with ambivalent
familiars, pacts with the wealth-
giving mother of these very deep
waters, through the twisted
mouths of the some-time meno-

paused "tricksters", spitting out
occult false promises. Within
such dominating folklore narra-
tives, why have you allowed
your serpentine form to be

tamed? By all means, your silent
death has ushered in another
level of inter-colonial trade. Your
populace, the so-called impo-
verished inhabitants of Ngxingxolo

have abandoned their altars and
their supplications conjured up
as mere fabrications in the
presence of the missionary God.
The water-bound angels and

serpentine creatures are up
and about courting destruction.

THE LAST SONG

Close to four decades now, I stand here, within
the walls of this museum, the image of your
wide open casket on display, your widow
clutching your heart with her very heart.

This last song, drenched with innumerable
pain and tears, cascading down those many
hills, 20 000 voices in unison, accompanying
you to the circle of your universal ancestors.

Bantubonke, tread well within the wide
circle of your forebears. That fateful
journey, Xhamela[2], naked and drenched
in blood and urine – brain damaged –

finally declared dead. Great lion of the
blood-stained landscapes of Tarkastad,
post-humously declared prophet, up to
the end, you fought. Security police,

like hungry vultures, scrabbling over
your drained body, determined only
to erase your gigantic strides, you still
fought. Gone too early, great lion

of our blood-ruined landscapes,

---

1. Xhamela is the Xhosa clan name for Steve Bantubonke Biko who on the 12th of September 1977 was killed in custody by South African security police.

slowly but surely they pinched
your intellect. Brain damaged,
 in the back of those classified
 vehicles,

black panther, they drove through
this very town, supposedly a hold
of those liberal charlatans.

HINTSA'S PORTRAIT

Through English picturesque, here
he stands. Overburdened with colonial
lexion, he still stands, an intransigent
opponent of colonial advance –
narrative of the war.

Possession of land through
nineteenth century Romantic
imagination – ceded territory.

Here he stands, as a figure
of Xhosa Royality. That only
through political manoeuvring,
Smith could be the true meaning
of a traitor.

Yet, this portrait cannot reflect
the realities of the many voices
still crying for a ceded throne,
Of which the climax was
the burning of Hintsa's kraal
and the mutilation of his body.

And even more, the exportation
of the king's head to the colonial
masters.

KING SHAKA OF THE ZULUS

I

King Shaka of the Zulus
Greatest son of Senzangakhona
Bred by the hills, raised by the lilies
Broke the Zulu sacrament.

II

Fed of fire and volcano
Iron man, Taurus
Zulu bull, bellowing
Raced with English bulls on the crooked paths
   of Nongoma.

III

Grazed on the racing hills of Langeni
Drank from the gushing streams of Khandempefu
Nguga, the sanctuary
Greatest son of Senzangakhona.

IV

Pastoral calf of the Zulu hills
Mushroom that shot out of the sun
Jewel hidden in the rocks of Stanger
Iron man, iron man.

V

Warlord, hailed death at its tracks
Tampered with the art of war
Led many to their momentous deaths
Iron man, iron man.

VI

King Shaka of the Zulus
Swallowed his own loins
Plundered, sucked the blood
Only to be swallowed by the red soils
    of Zululand.

VII

Hand in hand with Nomkhubulwane
To swallow the Zulu monarch
Shaka Zulu, Shaka Zulu
Greatest son of Senzangakhona.

VIII

Made love in blood chambers
Gave birth only through his fore-head
Traced the footsteps of Mjokwana
To the sunken Zulu throne.

IX

Iron sword, cutting the sinew
Fire sparks, grinding the bone,

Ochred blood, stealing the soul-
Greatest son of Senzangakhona.

X

Shaka Zulu, Brutus is coming!
The sons of Senzangakhona, heirs to the throne?
David and Goliath rearing their heads
Shake your iron robe and embrace the earth.

XI

Beloved of the Zulu gods
Even Zeus the Olympian
Fed by the ancient ravens
Shaka Zulu, Shaka Zulu.

QUESTIONS OF IDENTITY

Below me, a picturesque
valley, dotted, with undulating
hills. This valley, wanting to nestle
on the hills that I, dumbfounded,
wish to confide in.

Deep in these hills, I,
having rounded other heights,
more abstract than the guilt-inducing
panorama below my feet, I sense
inabilities, far beyond those of sight,

in defining this scenery. I saw
them sink, these grass thatched
domes, these corrugated iron
roofs. Upon the swift impact of this
view, I seem to trudge to an even higher

peak. Alone, shivering, I struggle
to locate any pathfinders.
Having confided all, in the secrecy
of these desolate hills – trusting
that no one would ever hear

my dark secrets – I walk down
to face more of my humiliation:
in this place, that only a higher
force knows why, I have decided
to call home. No matter how

sharp the contradictions that this
vulnerability confronts me with,
it is now – and only now –
that I absorb, with an even
sharper precision,
that what has been, has been –

the past almost shuts out
in the present. And even more,
that perhaps my presence
here is for other things, other
than those that seem to lodge
their claims.

RITES OF PASSAGE

Why should you always leave
us, unannounced? By the river's
bank, we could not see the stone
sinking, the fort from where
you spoke with the spirits. Only

the brim of your hair sailed
above the river's face. Shining,
the spirit world fused with
the waters –

we would not deliver you. And now
the timeless drums wish to lure
you back. Even the pigeons,
flocking upon these acacias, they
plead, relinquish yourself from
the river people.

The vigil dance, *intlombe*,
seems to be the only meeting
ground. The offerings we have
brought, the transient song
we murmur, as you fluently sing –
all melt into the seamless tune
of your doom: half-human,
half-spirit.

Upon your return,
we do not wish to see you
divine the end of our courses

in life, and perhaps foretell
a new beginning –
along shores foreign
to our memory.

We are much happy to be
who we are and the tides
that billow encroach
our enclosures in such
a merciless mode.

OSTRICH EGG CARRIER OF THE KALAHARI

Woman
Twenty ostrich eggs hang from your neck
Sinew net tied around your back
Holding you against yourself
Pressing you down.

The threads that run parallel
to your back
Patterned from dried-up leaves
From the African spear plant
Symbol of yoke and bondage
From your many life manifestations.

Like many children
Clinging to your back
Perforated ostrich eggs
Offspring of the hot Kalahari sands
Epicentre of eclipsed civilizations.

Twenty ostrich eggs
Full of reed-syphoned water
Vegetal twine plug sealing them off
Calabashes that you never drink from
Springs that never quench your thirst.

With their placentas dried up
Displaced embryos
That could never see their infancy
Still
Broken pieces pierced together.

Ornamental ostrich egg shell beads
Metamorphosing into dance rattles
Reserved for esoteric activities
Culminating into curative shaman songs
Tantalizing rain dances and trances

STRUGGLES OF MEMORY

Unaccountable crimes qualify one to exile
To die away from family and homeland

Coming safe to mainland, to light my fires
Is all I prayed for

Could I have hoped for a garden of remembrance
Where the grass-weed grew fast and tall?

There could be no garden of remembrance
As tributes due to the dead,

were not awarded. As the white skulls,
un-mourned, still peeped their husks

From the rock-sharpened surfaces. There is
no garden of remembrance

As the insistent hands of degrading memories
have erased the nation's essence –

As the skulls of the unnamed, undignified,
Still hang from their bleeding necks,

as if to curse the Xhosa eclipse
When all those who dared, ventured,

through darkness, into the unknown.

There is no garden of remembrance

Where the mind exhausted
Has lost its tenacity

DEATH WISH

Tell them I am dead,
To all the wishes of the dead.

The stars, the moon, what more?
No longer matter in my world.

Tell them I am dead,
Stone-dead, beneath the red-dotted sky.

The drizzling, down-pouring of the rain
Struggles to touch my sand-coarsened lips.

The winds that stride can no longer move me
The waves, the storms can no longer shake me.

I am dead,
Like a stone, amidst blazing flames.

I am dead,
To the songs sung by the ghosts of yesterday.

I am dead,
To the clinker of the spears and the shadows of the shields.

The goat, the groaning bull,
Is no redemptive equivalent:

I am dead also,
To the trickery of the foreign gods.

I will not mourn the black beauty.
I will not detest the white legacy.

TO HIMSELF

I

I find myself, on this bed,
Without a wife, my child gone,
My father miles away.

I have been to places
Where no mother's love
Could fetch me.

I have wandered,
Like a vagabond,
In and out of institutions.

The last time I was in Cape Town
I can't remember coming here,
Who I was, or what I was.

I know all
The psychiatric drugs by name:
Lithium, Lagatil, and others.

I have some disorder,
So I' m told, I'm bipolar,
Manic depression.

II

Here, in this city,
I walk, I suffer,

All the chains of consciousness.

Back here, in the country,
In the village where I was born,
It is no different too.

They say to me, my relatives,
Under that village sun, my father
Lived elsewhere: I never knew him.

I – it seems I will never now give her
The garden she longed for,
That my father, absent, never gave her.

I – I am nothing but
These vindictive spells,
This malady of mind and heart.

III

I watch others, all their virtues,
But to me
They have no value.

I hear all these words,
But to me
They have no meaning.

I was supposed to be among them,
An achiever, figurehead, success.
And today, where am I?

Again, on this bed,

Without a wife, a child,
With only this mind that races,
This heart that knows only
Its own illness.

HOMECOMING

The wooden door is broken, the roof thatch
Flags. The wind has fallen low. The clouds,
hiding behind our mountains, Amatolas,
seem deader than dead volcanoes.

And here I am – and here you are, mother,
Your dry hair burns in the winter sun.
Your face is pale today in its thin light.
Your hands, blistered, twist at your
Chapped lips.

Yes, I am home again. But where is the cow
Today, that would bellow as it calved?
And where is the horse that gallops as it
always did, from the crown of the hill?
There is only me, your son, who has come back.

Yes, you sent me away, into that other world.
It is ten years now; I have come home.
I kick the dust. My hands are empty.
My head spins, while you, silent,
bend to the fire.

Yes, you tried to bend me to your will.
You tried to make me one with the shades,
our ancestors. But, I feared those images;
I followed another light.
All you worshipped, I derided.
And still your silence is what I fear.
I kick the dust, unconsoled

by this old cooking spot, its ashes,
the charred, iron smell of the black pots.
Son and mother – we are back together

You, your cheeks as hollow now
as if you drank the wind,
And I, your child, whose stomach feels
horrified, knowing I am back at the beginning –

Here at home, where all guilt begins.

THE RETURN

Standing in the cold warmth of this sunset,
Hearing the primitive music of those birds again,
I see a world that stands only in its ashes:
Only some memories, of childhood, remain.

A place, encircled by low hills,
With its apparently fat cows and empty
green fields,
With the extravagant beauty of its mimosas –
This world is no longer mine.

Now, pop songs replace folklore.
History has supplanted legend.
Railway-lines have cut their tracks
through the ancient forests and goat paths.

A frontier once – a frontier still –
Blamed to Nongqawuse
Where we were maneuvered
to enact a blood scourge
on a peasant kingdom.

War of the Axe, War of Mlanjeni,
War of Nxele, War of Thuthula –
Here, at the heart of this old unrest,
This bloodshed,

I stand again, like one of those
first peoples who, the waters
of the Fish, the Khoisans' having failed,

Now must hunt amidst dry stone.

GENESIS

Once there was an epoch when
Women. Men, paced around, searching
the river, the seed, the stone-fire.
They ate the rich sap that lives
in the intestines of the roots.

Once upon a time, our fires burned
tall, their flames opening the darkness –
as we chanted. Dancing, we unveiled
the reservoirs of our light.

There, our feet tattooing, we chased
the moon. We chased the blue buck,
the eland. We raced with the San
and the Khoi – even as far as the red
pillars of the stormy skylines.

We watched our high priests, sangomas,
negotiating with clouds.
They called roots by name.
They traced and chased death
back to its black caves.

But, while we were busy
with our dancing, our vigil, our beer party,
a great serpent came, from out of the North.
He whisked his red tongue,
our village turned into ashes.
And still the poet sings, still
I make these verses, years later,
Even here, where no cowhide drum sounds,

so we may find that river, those footpaths.
So we might find again the seed, stone-fire.

DAYBREAK

This road, gravel rusted, coiling back upon itself,
takes me to a dam that splinters in the light once more.
Early morning: there is a hint of mountain light, of snow
about this water's shine. The small shrubs, yellow –
budded, warn of spring. But is all silent.

These hills, surrounding here, have survived
Many adversities, going back to Dias, centuries back,
to Nongqawuse, her prophecy, our disaster.
But nature, summer, winter, has her own resilience.

All around me, still, there sounds the history
That almost swallows me – the testimony of men, of women,
Children – all swallowed by the earth, its darkness,
Their bones now rattling under unattended graves.

But today, to me, these myths, that history,
Seem exhausted. Complacent, we are always blaming them,
Dias and his cross, Nongqawuse, her prophecy.
Now, only a tortoise, nerves frightened by my footfall,
turns back to the water, that door to the river,
the shimmer where sun first strikes its surface.

I walk alone this morning, without ancestors,
a river that cannot be tamed by any bridge,
I can see the forked fingers of the sunrise
Straightening towards me – a reed that,
Knocked flat by many storms, raises itself slowly
On this bank to seek a single sheath of light.

PRAYER

Eternal Spirit, lift us higher than the trees,
Make us see the fires beneath the earth.
Make us walk more slowly than our fleeting breath.
Plant us in your passages
Beyond sacrificial blood and wooden temples.

May we not be proud of the she-goats, the groaning bulls.
Make us see you walking with the river flowing,
Accompanying, as you used to do, the perished sun.
Make us believe that the mountain
Is also your child, and that the sea
Is the only sibling of the blue skies.

Eternal Spirit, help us assassinate the drought.
Even if death grows bigger than we are,
may we be in peace with Nongqawuse,
her mermaids. Help us, to make pain and love
our own. Instil in us your present,
your continuous knowledge

That you may cease to be that ghost
Whose existence pounds
The delicate floors of memory.

REFUSING TO WORSHIP

When darkness
had slipped down, the youth
would have to march out of
his wood and plastic hut
in the forest.

First in the entrance,
The wooden post whose two wide
Stretched arms pointed at two
Disputing roads, seemed to be

scrutinising his poignant
moves. The youth absorbed,
moved by the interrogative
stance taken by the silent
post, on his refusal

to worship. Frozen, his eyes
fixed on the red skylines
above the kraal, the youth
refuses to worship.

Many years later,
Confronted with the same
visions - fragments –
he is still much unable
to recognize just a single
gesture from those he regards
as just the silent.
pristine and forgotten.

Much bruised, his fingers
Cramped – still breathing
the African air – frantic,
he carries on with his
search.

MAINSTAY

An overnight mist – left-overs –
captured by the mountain, oozing
from its ridge-tightened lips,
seeking to move on. Pregnant clouds
summersaulting, a mimosa terrain

with its thorn scrub huddling
beneath gum trees. Plastic
huts protrude from a dense forest,
an asylum for circumcision school
candidates. Only if the landscape

could be true to such stories;
a blood-thirsty tradition that
always refuses to account for
its botched circumcisions.

Pricking bush, stone white –
very white – like Ezekiel's valley,
nerve-wrecking heights, hill
snoozing upon shoulder of higher
hill, shadows caught in limbo,
a mist crouching over –
climbing to the summit.

Swallows, citizens of many
Worlds now swarm this frantic
Landscape. My moods swing,
with the clouds, as they rise
and fall upon unknown village

and city, tumbling upon
foreign cultures. But, here
is my mainstay, here in
this land where the sound
of poetry struggles
to be.

The landscape, having given
birth to many children –
like bastard offspring – seems
indifferent. After all, it
is in this landscape only
that one can trust, having
survived us all. Still,
when our stories desert us,
she is the one that embraces
them, and even us.

NAMING YOUR LOSS

You have spent well beyond a decade
Suckling from the breasts of foreign lands,
And its people have put on your lap
other languages that confronted
by the flat consonants of the vernacular
you are found weeping. Imagine, a native,
upon return having to guess what you
once looked like. And the girls and boys,

former playmates, frown at the sight of such
a hopeless picture. The women's sighs, the
weeping of the rain and all about this place
that once absorbed you, like a spouse
entangled to a love-fearing partner, roll
backwards with every footstep you take –
towards the interior. Being not so dull,
imagine, discovering how useless you are

here, where belonging and continuity
seem to be commodities. Now tired –
understandably, the landscape has
been altered and young generations
have taken over – the mind seeks
refuge but left to wander on the
delicate borders of the wind.
Wretched, you retreat back

to those other places where
you had always known that you
never belonged, only that proving
others wrong was all you sought.

Your dilemma is that of a wounded
Bird, upon discovering the blight
Around its nestling ground. Name
your loss:
this is your only possession.

THE VILLAGE CARNIVAL

The village carnival, dancers
Move their sinuous thighs as they
advance from hill to hill. I call
it such, these disenfranchised
celebrations with pain,

a phantom of the past. I used
to know it as such, when far
away we could hear its music
and run for safety in the company
of its offerings. A marathon,

we recklessly threw ourselves
in the mercies of its swing,
till one clear morning – if we
were lucky – we would be aware
that some higher force had
cheated us. I am

addressing you in the past
tense for such reasons:
that perhaps the magic never
did exist. Even if I cannot

really work it out;
something has happened
and the village carnival still
shouts as it did when,
undefiled, I could still answer.

MEDITATING

I have thought so much
about another boy who used to pass
through here. With tender sunrays
still struggling to split out,
he used to define each activity –
only through what his forebears
dictated.

He used to wake up
pregnant with dreams of the land's
plenty. When his poems could
only be sung – he did not give them
such name then – to the beasts
that defined such a life, the summer's
sequel used to scatter him and fed him –
spoils of the African landscape.
Paralysed by the gleam of the
corn's beard, he would hardly
think of the blood and tears
that have gone down.

And now
I wonder if perhaps this same
boy has moved on to another
village, on a higher ground than
ours. As I am struggling
to recover from the blow of his
persuasions, I wonder still,
why is it that world
only strikes me as a life

modelled only after death?

A REMINDER

think of me
when the country
and the city seem
to be pointing
fingers at each other
as if they were servants
serving different masters.

It was my theme.

think of me
when these two great
forces that work behind
the scenes of our lives
lay their bruising
claims on the object:
an image, of my poetry.

When they bang and hit
The mystery object; my
Image helplessly caught
In between beyond any
point of recognition.

It is still my theme.

think of me
when the country hobbles
around to greet the city.

-I would never say such.

the dreams of the
blazing flames projected
towards the city trouble
my mind, the hope of a
damned hell posthumously
awarded to the 'troubled'
village is a big joke.

-This would never be my dream.

think of me
when two simple humans
struggle to hear each other.

I persist,
It is my theme:

when the country and
the city fail to recognize
the earth which will
always be the common
factor.

AT THE END OF THE JOURNEY

Will I lift up my hands
And scatter the shrilling bones
that lured me
The word of the stinking cowhide
drum
The gulping of the dead legions?

I sought to be a cannibal
I built walls, I set bridges
I wanted to see myself –
Reflected
In the gleam of the dead tree
And the satiric movement
of the water.

My chants were only sung
To raise myself above disorders
That only issues of predisposition
Could lay claim on.

Now, my demons play tricks
On my mind
The dead heroes I incited –
Theirs was a glory
never mine
An honour long sunk
In the dark sands of history.

Wind-whipped, I have to turn
my head backwards

The journey has ended
There are no more miles
to cover.

The fingers of my mind
will have to curl inwards
I will have to be content
that in the dark secrets
of history,
my mind has no share.

TO STEPHEN WATSON

Wordsmith of particular note,
you departed without letting
me know. As your last born
I thought I would be the first
one to know, still I would have
slid through the coast,
to your Citadel and brought
you aloe branches. Sleep tight,
send me a greeting to Homer.
Poet Laureate, you departed
before your craft could bloom.

Keep on, scribe your words
on that granite stone.
I will scatter your ashes
on your love nest –
the scary light of the
Cedarbergs.

SCATTERED FEATHERS

The only evidence of your departed
presence is this august presence,
the scattered feathers. Seemingly,
you have gone on to join the train
of those departed before you who
have gone missing; and still upon
putting my magnifying glasses on
these leftovers – reaching out my
fingers to be able to own your absence,
yes, you are indeed an ancestor now,
my true saint. My dear, you are gone
now, as a true martyr of this cause –
how could I – in the haunting presence
of these scattered feathers ever
commit the mistake of pointing
my fingers backwards?

LAND OF THORNS

Giving up on my escapades
Not only my hands and feet bruised
A breath that I can no longer hold
Dragging behind, all the offspring
        I could never inherit.

Walking away, I could never imagine
That carefully sandwiched between
        many memories
Could only linger baskets of amnesia.

Beneath your laps still lie
The whistle of the winds that can only
drive me back to the lure
        of the land of thorns.

When all I have been chasing has just
        been one moment ahead of
Every footstep I could ever take.

With every drop of water falling down
Beneath these strange mountains
A line of tear attributed to my fears
Has fallen down, I have lost count of
        the moments.

Like a defeated child
Coming back to embrace a consumed
        embryo
Mine could only be a journey in circles.

Never to reach a destination point
And never to own a defined territory.

THE CAPTURED MAIDEN

By early sunrise this day
I should have long deserted this place.
The spaces far away
Together with my people
Have long forgotten the sight of me.
Early in the days of my womanhood
I left, in search of your kraal.

Many moons have I counted
The glimmering light consuming
Many by the weary banks of the river pool
Where, as first born of your kraal,
I have been master
Of your many ceremonies.

Legions
Long have they deserted you
Big piles of herbs their awards
Crowds behind them
Countless herds scattered
Throughout those sleeping valleys.

Patterning yourself after your predecessors
You suffocated me with your misplaced proverbs
The traditional conclave –
Your main residence
Has lost its relevance.

It is almost a hundred moons now
With me tendering your cattle

And me creating your music
Slouching with your medicinal bag
Over my tattered shoulders.

My defeated husband
Has long forgotten
The warmth of my now tired breasts.
I have to please your kindred
With all that I am.

The members of my clan
And those of my traded-in man
Have long been calling me
Through many dreams –
Gushing words from beyond.

With your baboon fly-whisk
And your chameleon head-gear
Have you shrugged their wishes
I could only own
Countless drums of my tears.

Today
I would like you to know
The contents of my last dream
Which I could not pour
Over your stone ears –
To leave you, unseen
For you would never release me.

Have I not paid enough
For the dream that brought me here?
Come, let us dance

For the last time now.

IN THE MEMORY OF MAKHANDA

Now that you have left, and two centuries
Have sought refuge in the mystery
Of the many cascading moons,
If given a chance I could not even
Pick you out from a crowd.

Who am I?
But a little worm
Baked beneath the misty NtabakaNdodas
The Amalindas, a battle-fort
For the many regiments after you
In defence of the land, the old curse
That has driven many to war
Are a pebble-throw away from where
The many creased hands
Have pushed the dry *phutu*
Into my mouth.

Growing up, toiling the land
Of my predecessors
With these mountain slopes
Shadowing me
From the many pains I bore
And the many rainfalls
That were imprinted
On my existence
I never could have known
That many centuries ago a giant
Was raised by the Khoisan queen
And a mystic-priest conversed

With the mountain-god.

I hear that one day at the prime
Of your magic days
Ordered by the great queen
You decided to desert
All the comfort you knew
In the mountains.

I say so, for you were the self-made
King of the forests
And the magician who resided
In the caves
The creator of Tai.

You marched down, and embraced
The pains of your people.
Not only that, you were
On the battle line
And never feared,
And never moved.

Why have they erected
sanctuaries
And monuments on our land?
As if we willingly handed
The land to them
As a peace offering.
After all that, it was not enough
Blood, bones, betrayal.

Colonial harbinger, only if I could
Have a lasting view

Of those crumbled palaces you
sought to defend
And the gothic kings who sat
On the sunk ivory thrones.

My lines are only fed by cries
From a forced out generation
Two centuries after your calculated
Dismissal.

Great carrier of spear,
I need to let go
Of your blood-tainted rag
I found scattered
On these ghostly Gompo beaches
As King Mgolombane is summoning me
To the old citadel on the hills
Of the long-winding Amatola mountain ranges.
The python whose feet are
The roaring waves of the Indian Ocean
And whose pillows are hidden
In the caves, below the feet
Of Table Mountain.

In my sleep, King Mgolombane
Has shown me
Sacred herbs to dig, revered
Animal skins to collect
For the festivities of the great king
Are looming
And the lure of the virgin dance
Has re-possessed me.

MY FATHER'S SPEAR

In search of my father's line
of lineage, unravelled - with
such dexterity - indelible clues
are carefully packed on
the path of chaotic discovery.

A non-existent kraal, a long
sunk mud rondavel whose
stick-bricks have long returned
to their primitive existence.
The bee-hive roof, imagined

only as testimony of primitive
residence, long swallowed
by the hungry rocks carrying only
green moss robed mud-dew.
This land of Spirit, the Place

of Thorns, so was it named by
those ancient warriors driven
away by a primitive version of
colonial rebut, is nowhere
to be found. Its people, too,

quintessentially from land and
place, whose footsteps have been
swallowed by the quick sands
accumulative in their fronts,
whose descendants only have

inherited a movement of loss –
identity and throne. Their precedents,
as they negotiated with the loss
of existence, deserted their
benevolent spirits baptized

assegais and spears, leaving
the long collection of bullock
horns scattered about - fleeing
from many regiments who only
saw through the eye of the sword,

now exiled in rocky places and
mountainous slopes invite me
to carry their fallen spears on my
shoulders and claim the scattered
bullock horns. In this unending

search for land and precedent,
the only visible remnant is a spear-
like rod that visits me only at night,
hanging from two poignant poles.
I wish to hold it, but no one could

perform such an act, its last custodian –
like my father - had left with no
trace of existence. The incense,
the only negotiating ground
with the departed spirits,

tendering me to the sword,
that is my preferred verb, until
one day I chose to hold it, out

of desperation, once again that
line of lineage having deserted me,

and there I was, seeking to retrace
their non-existent footsteps. In my
own ways, I had to retrieve my father's
haunting spear, a gateway to an already
forgotten way of life, from my own

personalized vistas of dream-carved
memories, and pronounce once again,
that I was seeking to be a man after
the long line of lineage which made
my father the man who I was supposed
to be, a prototype of a man I hardly knew.

A LETTER TO THUTHULA

Whe Thuthula!, I have come to your place of worship,
our little *sivivana*, named after you. Carved deep in our
individual memories, is your imaginary statue, you
Cleopatra of our pastoral land. You should be there
girl, amongst those thorn-crowned bushes,
just above the now dry and filthy Xhukwana
stream.

In my hand are beautiful beads weaved
with my very hands, from our colours,
to continue building your crown that
enchanted those two men hungry
for love. This is the only thing I have,
enchanting queen of our land. I should
have slaughtered a white cow,

calabashes drowned in white foam
should be dominating this place with
their sorghum-smell. I do not own a
crystal-glowing beaker, where I could
shake *ubulawu*, to invoke your presence,
as the only transit to your imaginary

palace, far beyond those tall *Mhlontlo*
trees, in a land far far away, where the
stoic Qamata forever rules.
Madlamini, whose services could even
bring those stubborn chiefs and kings
to my presence, right now, demands

a cow, which for me is another luxury
my father's house alone could never
afford, for such a service should be
accorded by women from all walks
of our broken kingdom. I am here now,
to address you as a caring mother,

for the troubles are too many.
Whe ntombi! I still find it hard to comprehend,
how on earth did you ever do it? *Girl power girl,
girl power.* The famous love triangle, that
brought out sharp spears from the royal
house, is still a defining epitome.

And still, after you waged the war
of the Xhosa monarchies, they ate right from
your hand, here in our pastoral land all
the girls are queuing up for the slaughtering
machine of the present day imported
monarchy.

And still, one last question, was it you
first or Nongqawuse? Whoever could
be the predecessor, your *girl power* -
combined, still encircles our necks
with chains of slavery. Be a true Cleopatra,
please turn the monarch's noses to the

other direction, towards our diminishing
pastoral land and our silent suffering.

WHEN I USED TO DREAM

The skies would push their blue covers
away. Spear-holding warriors would
descend the far-away hills and claim
their existence on my lowly kraal.
My grass mat would ascend the
misted Amatola's, with my spear
in my hand would I come. Sitting
below those grey-haired olive trees,
together we would converse, once
again burning with their fire would
I descend to the more reluctant pastoral
populace. Carrying that light, their light,
I would transverse through every hill.

But now, exiled from the populace,
supposedly speaking posthumously –
my claim is on nothing, as that
ancient wisdom only belongs to
those trillions of years gone by,
that only a candid eye of a sage
could transcend, only when I used
to dream.

THE MAIDEN RETURNS

Sleeping hills of my people
I awaken you
Only in the name of a dream that sent me
    away
I come, I come
Aware of the absence of my clan
I wish only to narrate my story
To these hills that remained faithful
    to your enduring presence
Earnestly have they sat here
For all these many moons of my absence
I can only burn my incense
As the essence of my home-coming
And shake my beaker
Captivated by its magical foam
As the only kernel of my father's kraal
As those I had to come back to
Have long left in my absence
My trade belongs and is owned by such
The benevolence that stands out
    the test of time, like
this enduring landscape
Perhaps
That was the only reason of my exile
To learn to master the art of communicating
With all the members of my clan
The living, the dead and the long forgotten.

VOICES FROM WITHIN

Hail you princess
Who could not rest in the wake of a dream
A foaming drum awaits you
Unseen by your naked eyes
A roaring bull greets you
Just above your tired hands
The robes you forsook
Running away from your strangler
Are being weaved by tireless hands.
As masters and dispatchers of your dream
We send to you love
In all its possible meanings
A beaker endowed with the magic
Of your own people
And those of your in-laws
Under whose influence you ran away
A tiger skin is ready
To cover your nakedness.
The eye of wisdom cannot see
Where human fault presides
We give to you what is yours.

PRAYER TO ULU (AFTER CHINUA ACHEBE'S ARROW OF GOD)

Inside my *obi*, I have laid an imaginary shrine
Ivory skulls of your great lineage of high priests
Dangle above my troubled fore-head
Great Ulu of the Igbo clan.

Long long long ago
When lizards were in ones and twos
Our forefathers carved you
King-god of our six kingdoms.

To you, we cry Great Ulu
The one who single-handedly saved us
From the tyranny of a vampire-god
In supplication to you, I break
    my last kola.

Being of the Sky's first weeping
Is our yam harvest going to be reduced
    to tinder?
Your high priest refuses to break
    these two kolas
A threshold to a new season of plenty.

Is it not your high priest?
Who chose to elope for two full moons?
With the mirage of the foreign gods?
Must we die, must we die of hunger?

Our medicine men's goat-skin bags
    have run out of camwood
The fire that flickers through the night
    vigil
Will never wake us from our bamboo
    beds
Great Ulu of the Igbo clan.

I can hear a solitary voice –
the tampering of the foreign gods
For how long must we delay
    our second burials?
And the melody accompanying
    the yam feast festivals
Retrace your footsteps,

From the journey to oblivion.

AT THE GATES OF XHOSALAND

At the gates of Xhosaland we have come, empty handed
we stand. From far away we come, with imaginary
landscapes as the only precursors of our path. Plenty,
glorious kingdoms and chieftaincies have we been
promised. At the gates of Xhosaland, the only thing

our bone fingers can lay their hold on are non-existent
graves, deep-dug on caves that are hidden from
anybody's sight, buried by the rushing of pastoral
armies from civilisations gone by. Imprints on the
sand-stones that desperately hold on crumbled
granite stone offer themselves as only a clue-

to the crumbled kingdoms of the original inhabitants
of this ghost land, not the Xhosaland originally
tendered to us. Red-pitched pillars from dust derived
ochre, only hanging from man carved memories.
Big-bellied men, self-appointed custodians of this
pristine land, now in ashes, only tender to us pieces
of history only to sabotage our thinking abilities.

Here we find no solace, only retreat back to the
trillions of years that claim our only existence.

We can only come back, only as ghosts that
haunt carefully packed archives – well crafted
non-truths themselves. Glittering museums
abounding the land only could crumble in
the face of our haunting questions, we reinvent

ourselves and carve new professions, digging ugly truths hidden in this land. We still revisit those grave-caves with now abandoned kings and chiefs, on whose thrones now sit man and women whose blood has no lineage to them. We go back, with our heads banging on us, in fear of the most famous word – 'treason' and its equivalent 'prison'. We go back to assume our spirit-world existence, where no such fears exist.

THE LEO MARQUARD NECKTIE

They gave you to me
as an award – for service –
a sense of belonging.

Now you hang round
my neck as if
there hung from you

those years, that other world,
a university, a residence,
a place where I

first learnt
to give up
my childhood,

where I knew
how it was to be swallowed
into elusive kinds of love.

Lately I take
my solo walks
through these dark streets,

that were once a setting
for my idealistic escapades
a child's naivety.

Everyday I wipe
my mouth so dry,

with my dirty right hand,
trying to wipe away
a world yours,
I hoped to forget.

Yet your big blue wedge
stares at me from this mirror
where I stand.

A neck-tie,
circling my neck,
that lasso

of the other world,
still tightening around my throat,
as if it were a noose.

NOMTSHWEBELELE'S STONE

By the river's side it lays,
deep in the running waters
it rears up its head, its shining
surface standing like a throne
for the spirits. Standing on
the bank of the riverside,
addressing the ancient spirits
it waves its hand towards me,
the crab watches over, laughing
at me.

Back at my maternal
home, the ancient homestead,
this big stone was disturbed
from its sleep amongst my
grandmother's possessions
that had long returned to
the earth's compost, maybe
her long pipe, maybe her beaded
necklaces and maybe the isacholo
she passed on to my grandfather
on the eve of their courting. This
huge stone, together with a rusted
coin from Mozambique, now lost,

are the only prized possessions
I found on Nomtshwebelele's site,
the grandmother I never had
a privilege to see. This huge stone,
still sleeps silently next to the

rondavel I built at the same spot

where Nomtshwebelele's rondavel
sunk after a mysterious fire.

This must have been her
grinding stone, or maybe
a throne where she sat when
she communed with the long
dead spirits, while enhaling
her long pipe, if she had one,
and carefully counting her
ornamental beads carefully
scattered through her body.

AT EVENING

That line where dark and light converge, where stone and sky would seem to meet. There are times I've tried to chart, to name it as it wavers, God's angry light still pouring in, darkness in the east encroaching, conquering all. Many's the evening I have waited in that place where it was never clear- at least to me if I should turn, left or right, north or south, whether that sunset light was God's own glory or only the halo of a larger emptiness. I know that He once came to Job in that moment of moments, apologising for making him His guinea pig, thanking Job for being the man who had released Him from moral bondage to human race. But I know I can't be Job, that my own darkness can't surpass his. I know, since Job's day on that ash-heap, God was not obliged to shower His followers with manna. And yet, at evening, I still watch that line where dark and light converge-while a city, lights emerging, begins to flourish, its mountain slowly vanquished. I still wait, wondering what its name could be, what God might call it, that line, shifting, that runs through my life?

MAMLAMBO

Steeped into your deep
presence, the citadel
whose unity with the
morning light leaves
vestiges of your temple
in the abiding presence
of the river's eye.
Nzwakazi, leave me
be, while I compose
this song of rejection
dedicated to you, the
water muse. I would
not wish my sight
to let go of me as I
silently stand on
these slippery water
banks. In tandem with
the horrifying dance
of the wind-shaken
reeds, I whisper,
leave me be most
beautiful girl. I can
never climax into a
moment of intimacy
within your sharp
breasts. The symphony

of death, intertwined
within your ghostly
presence, is an over-

casting shadow over my own existence. Holder of the rain queen's stone, step out from your magic horse and reclaim the other world where your crystal ball is intricately hidden. The tragic fables that you spit through the river's mouth could never orchestrate a melody of content for me.

Mmap New African Poets Series

If you have enjoyed *Ntombentle: Selected Poems,* consider these other fine books in the **Mmap New African Poets** Series from *Mwanaka Media and Publishing:*

I Threw a Star in a Wine Glass by Fethi Sassi
Best New African Poets 2017 Anthology by Tendai R Mwanaka and Daniel Da Purificacao
Logbook Written by a Drifter by Tendai Rinos Mwanaka
Mad Bob Republic: Bloodlines, Bile and a Crying Child by Tendai Rinos Mwanaka
Zimbolicious Poetry Vol 1 by Tendai R Mwanaka and Edward Dzonze
Zimbolicious Poetry Vol 2 by Tendai R Mwanaka and Edward Dzonze
Zimbolicious: An Anthology of Zimbabwean Literature and Arts, Vol 3 by Tendai Mwanaka
Under The Steel Yoke by Jabulani Mzinyathi
Fly in a Beehive by Thato Tshukudu
Bounding for Light by Richard Mbuthia
Sentiments by Jackson Matimba
Best New African Poets 2018 Anthology by Tendai R Mwanaka and Nsah Mala
Words That Matter by Gerry Sikazwe
The Ungendered by Delia Watterson
Ghetto Symphony by Mandla Mavolwane
Sky for a Foreign Bird by Fethi Sassi
A Portrait of Defiance by Tendai Rinos Mwanaka
Zimbolicious: An Anthology of Zimbabwean Literature and Arts, Vol 4 by Tendai Mwanaka and Jabulani Mzinyathi
When Escape Becomes the only Lover by Tendai R Mwanaka

وَيَسْهَرُ اللَّيْلُ عَلَى شَفَتِي...وَالغَمَام by Fethi Sassi
A Letter to the President by Mbizo Chirasha
This is not a poem by Richard Inya
Pressed flowers by John Eppel
Righteous Indignation by Jabulani Mzinyathi:
Blooming Cactus by Mikateko Mbambo
Rhythm of Life by Olivia Ngozi Osouha
Travellers Gather Dust and Lust by Gabriel Awuah Mainoo
Chitungwiza Mushamukuru: An Anthology from Zimbabwe's Biggest Ghetto Town by Tendai Rinos Mwanaka
Zimbolicious: An Anthology of Zimbabwean Literature and Arts, Vol 5 by Tendai Mwanaka
Because Sadness is Beautiful? by Tanaka Chidora
Of Fresh Bloom and Smoke by Abigail George
Shades of Black by Edward Dzonze
Best New African Poets 2020 Anthology by Tendai Rinos Mwanaka, Lorna Telma Zita and Balddine Moussa
This Body is an Empty Vessel by Beaton Galafa
Between Places by Tendai Rinos Mwanaka
Best New African Poets 2021 Anthology by Tendai Rinos Mwanaka, Lorna Telma Zita and Balddine Moussa
Zimbolicious: An Anthology of Zimbabwean Literature and Arts, Vol 6 by Tendai Mwanaka and Chenjerai Mhondera
A Matter of Inclusion by Chad Norman
Keeping the Sun Secret by Mariel Awendit
وسِيجِلٌّ مَكْتُوبٌ لَتَائِه by Tendai Rinos Mwanaka
Ghetto Blues by Tendai Rinos Mwanaka
Zimbolicious: An Anthology of Zimbabwean Literature and Arts, Vol 7 by Tendai Rinos Mwanaka and Tanaka Chidora
Best New African Poets 2022 Anthology by Tendai Rinos Mwanaka and Helder Simbad
Dark Lines of History by Sithembele Isaac Xhegwana

a sky is falling by Nica Cornell
Death of a Statue by Samuel Chuma
Along the way by Jabulani Mzinyathi
Strides of Hope by Tawanda Chigavazira
Young Galaxies by Abigail George
Coming of Age by Gift Sakirai
Mother's Kitchen and Other Places by Antreka. M. Tladi
Best New African Poets 2023 Anthology by Tendai Rinos Mwanaka, Helder Simbad and Gerald Mpesse
Zimbolicious Anthology Vol 8 by Tendai Rinos Mwanaka and Mathew T Chikono
Broken Maps by Riak Marial Riak
Formless by Raïs Neza Boneza
Of poets, gods, ghosts. Irritants and storytellers by Tendai Rinos Mwanaka
Ethiopian Aliens by Clersidia Nzorozwa
In The Inferno by Jabulani Mzinyathi
Who Told You To Be God by Mariel Awendit
Nobody Loves Me by Abigail
The Stories of Stories by Nkwazi Mhango
Nhorido by Siphosami Ndlovu and Tinashe Chikumbo
Best New African Poets 10th Anniversary: Selected English African Poets by Tendai Rinos Mwanaka
Best New African Poets 10th Anniversary: Interviews and Reviews of African Poets by Tendai Rinos Mwanaka
Best New African Poets 10th Anniversary: African Languages and Collaborations by   Tendai Rinos Mwanaka
ANTOLOGIA DOS MELHORES "NOVOS" POETAS AFRICANOS 10° Aniversário: Poetas Africanos Da Língua Portuguesa Selecionados by Lorna Telma Zita and Tendai Rinos Mwanaka
ABRACADABRA, by Olivia Ngozi Osuoha
DES MEILLEURS "NOUVEAUX" POÈTES AFRICAINS

10ᵉ Anniversaire : Poètes africains d'expression française by Geraldin Mpesse and Tendai Rinos Mwanaka
Taurai Amai by Cosmas Tasvika Manhanhanha
Nhemeramutupo by Oscar Gwiriri